Right Livelihood:
the Twelve Ethics of Work

by

David Thomas, PhD

Fifty-Sixth Street Press – Kansas City/Omaha

Copyright © 2025 by David Thomas, PhD

All rights reserved. No part of this publication may be reproduced, stored in a retrieval system, or transmitted, in any form or by any means, electronic, mechanical, photocopying, recording, or otherwise, without the prior written permission of the author.

ISBN: 9780578710822

Distributed by IngramSpark and Fifty-Six Street Press

Cover art: Paula Ziegman

Cover design: David Thomas

This book is one of several materials that make up the Ethics of Human Development Training Program. My hope is that this book can be of use to individuals of all ages, particularly high school and college students about to enter the world of work. D. Thomas

For Ronald Dwain Smith
1921 - 1990

*and for all those who seek the opportunity
that work affords.*

Acknowledgments

I am very grateful to the following individuals for reading earlier versions of this manuscript and for offering suggestions for its improvement: David Shrader, Phil Minkin, Jon Levin, Dan Dancer, Don Jennings, Terry Kempf, Jay Williamson, R. Ross Gipple, Gordon Becker, Don Stilson, and Paula Ziegman.

I also would like to acknowledge the work of certain writers whose work has influenced me greatly; in particular, John David Garcia and R. Buckminster Fuller. Garcia's books, *The Moral Society* and *Creative Transformation*, impressed me deeply with their power and clarity. His identification of the ethics required for creative and evolutionary advance along with his analysis of the relationship of ethics to bureaucracy are brilliant accomplishments to which this book owes a great deal.

Fuller remains one of the unacknowledged intellectual giants of the Twentieth Century. It was Fuller who, after fifty years of careful study, concluded that humanity's future depends not on scientific discovery or on governmental or religious structure but rather, and above all, on the integrity of each individual. When he wrote about ethics, as he did in *Critical Path*, he did so with great insight and precision.

Finally, my thanks to John Thomas, Jay Williamson, VPR Productions, Burt & Betty Thomas, and R. Ross Gipple for their generous support during the writing of this book.

—David Thomas, PhD
February 2025

Note to the Reader

Dear Reader,

You will have to decide if the ethics discussed in this book are relevant to you and your situation. The world of work is changing. Entire industries are vanishing while others are emerging. Automation, robotics, and AI are eliminating vast numbers of jobs. Even if your work performance is exemplary, you may find yourself out of work with little in the way of prospects. And there is no doubt some jobs, many perhaps, that hardly leave any time to do other than exactly what is prescribed by the job, itself. Little time available, for example, to consider how you might creatively serve or further improve your job and/or workplace (as the ethics of right livelihood invite you to do).

Still, there are many workplaces and many jobs where the ethics discussed will be relevant. Relevant in part because the ethics of right livelihood are as much in service to the individual who embraces them as they are to his or her workplace. For that reason, I invite you to consider these ethics carefully. If they are not relevant to your situation, then use them like a whetstone against which to sharpen and refine your own ethics.

Finally, lest there be any confusion, the ethics discussed in this book are not just for the employee but for the employer, as well; not just for the front-line worker but for the engineer, the salesperson, the information technology specialist, the accountant, the administrative staff, the CEO.

—David Thomas, PhD
February 2025

Background

It finally occurred to me when I was eleven or twelve. I was with my uncle, riding in his pick-up across one of the pastures on his farm. "How is it possible?" I asked. "I mean, horses don't get married, pigs don't get married. How can they have babies? People get married and they have babies. I understand that. But pigs and horses don't get married. So how does it work?"

My Uncle asked if I had talked to my father about this. "About what?" I asked. He then drove in circles, crisscrossing the countryside as he told me, thoroughly and with care, the facts of life. I had no idea.

What follows is an imaginary dialogue between a young man, perhaps in his early twenties, and his uncle. The topic is work or, more exactly, a specific way of working, a way that brings advantage both to the individual who practices it and the organization of which he or she is a part. It is a topic no less fundamental than the one I discussed with my uncle years ago.

The ethics that are the focus of this dialogue are called the ethics of human development. Though they may seem demanding at first glance, they do offer much in return. With these ethics the individual furthers his or her development as a person while at the same time serving the interests of both workplace and society. For these reasons, the ethics of human development can also be called <u>the ethics of right livelihood</u>.

When my uncle told me the facts of life, I did feel—along with the amazement—that an important veil had been lifted. Suddenly, I was in on the secret that turned out to be no secret at all. I was enlightened. What I was to do with this knowledge was up to me but, by all rights, I was—from that point—without excuse. Instead, I was conscious of "how things worked" and thus, in a position to be responsible for my acts.

My hope is that the dialogue that follows can serve the same end with respect to the ethics, art, and nature of work.

—David Thomas, PhD
February 2025

Right Livelihood:

working in a way that expands awareness, reduces suffering, refines character...

a way of working that leads to one's full human maturity...

that serves the best interests of both individual and larger community, part and whole.

It had been another difficult morning for young Mr. Patchet. His situation at work had worsened and things were starting to get out of hand. He needed a break, a walk instead of lunch to collect his thoughts.

How long had it been, he wondered to himself, since he had looked forward to his work? In recent months he had felt his motivation ebbing away, his desire to participate—let alone excel—waning. Was he somehow responsible for the dissatisfaction he felt? Had he gotten off track? Or was he now, and at last, merely awakening to the harsh reality of the work-a-day world?

Young Mr. Patchet was lost in his thoughts, his preoccupation such that he failed to notice the man hailing him from across the street. It was, he realized as the man drew near, his beloved Uncle whom he had not seen in years.

"Nephew," cried the uncle, as they embraced, "why the long face? The whole world got you down?"
"No, no, Uncle. It's my work. Please...my apologies. It's wonderful to see you."

The two men strolled, catching each other up on the events of recent years. There had been much that had transpired in both of their lives, and both were eager to hear the details. It didn't take them long to find their stride.

"So, tell me," the Uncle inquired at last, "what is the problem with this work of yours? It can't be that bad. You're employed and these are difficult times. I'm sure there are those who would be delighted to trade places with you."

"Yes, I know," replied his nephew. "And I am grateful to be employed. It's just that I thought it would be different than it is."

Young Mr. Patchet explained to his uncle that he had not found fulfillment in his work; rather than satisfaction, he had found office politics, the hoarding of personal power, disgruntlement and malaise.
"I was not prepared for the world of work, at least as I have it now," he concluded. "I was naïve. That's all I'm saying."

"'The world of work'", his uncle repeated. "Maybe you don't know how to work," he said. "Many people don't, you know."

"What do you mean, Uncle? Most people do know how to work, or so it seems to me. They spend their lives doing it."

"In my opinion," replied his uncle earnestly, "many people waste their lives at work, and they do so simply because they do not know how to work, not fully and to their own advantage. They know how to put in their time, that's true. They know how, in general, to get by but they do not know how to make their work 'work' for them. It's one of the reasons so many people feel dissatisfied with their work. No, Nephew, the dissatisfaction you describe is not yours alone. It's very widespread."

Young Mr. Patchet had never heard his uncle express this view. Not that it seemed unreasonable; indeed, he could imagine how it might be so. Still, it surprised him.

"Well, then, Uncle, what about you? Do you know how to work?"

"Yes, I do," he replied. "But it took me many years, and many false starts."

"Then tell me. Save me the trouble. What is the secret?"

"There's no secret," his uncle replied. "Most work can be honorable. It depends largely on how you go about it. The trick is to make sure that you get what you need while, at the same time, fulfilling—if not exceeding—the needs and requirements of those for whom you work. To work in any other way will lead to the disillusionment you now feel."

Young Mr. Patchet considered his uncle's comment. "I'm not sure it's possible," he said after some thought. "With all due respect, Uncle, it seems to me that my needs and my employer's needs are often at odds. And sometimes deeply so."

"Sometimes, perhaps." replied the uncle. "But more often than not, your needs and your employer's needs are the same. If you were the employer—and some day you might be—I would say the same thing. At the deepest level, your needs are the same."

"If that is so, Uncle—and for the sake of discussion I'll grant that it is—then how can I, or anyone for that matter, work so that the needs of both parties are met?"

"More than anything else," his uncle replied, "it has to do with ethics, but in a way far more specific than most people realize."

Both men could see that their topic required more time than either had available; yet, each was eager to continue. "Come to the country this weekend," said the uncle. "Make a day of it. I can't remember when you last visited."

Young Mr. Patchet was thrilled. His Uncle's invitation meant that he would travel north, through countryside he loved. It meant that he would spend the day with his uncle, a wry and philosophical man who had always had his nephew's interests at heart. And it meant that he would have the opportunity to discuss the problem of work, the ethics of work, work at a deeper level, as his uncle seemed to suggest. Young Mr. Patchet relished the thought.

The week passed quickly, and soon young Mr. Patchet was on his way, riding through countryside he had not seen in years. It brought back a flood of memories.

"Welcome," greeted his uncle as young Mr. Patchet arrived. "I thought you might like to go for a walk. It's a beautiful day and it's been a long time since you've traipsed this countryside of ours."

His Uncle was right. The years away at school followed by the demands of finding and adjusting to work had kept him away. He could not remember spending time on his uncle's land except as a boy.

After a mile or so, they arrived at the pond where young Mr. Patchet had learned to skip rocks. To the South was a view of the entire valley. The two men relaxed and enjoyed the view.

Finally, young Mr. Patchet broke the silence. "Before leaving town, I looked up the word 'ethics.' According to the dictionary, it has to do with standards of conduct, the principles that govern your behavior...your duty to do what is right for individuals and society and to avoid what is wrong."

"Yes," responded his uncle, "That's correct. But I would add what the Japanese have to say about ethics. Their term for ethics, *rinri*, translates as 'human logic'[1] and in my view that adds an important element to the definition, especially when it comes to work.

"Human logic, Uncle?"

"Yes," his uncle replied, "guidelines or rules for educating, maturing and enlightening yourself. That's what I take the phrase to mean."

"That's quite a mouthful, Uncle... rules for educating, maturing and enlightening yourself."

"It's about an approach to work, Nephew; an approach to life, really. To work in accord with the ethics that embody human logic educates you. It teaches you about your work and about how to work, but it also teaches you about yourself. It matures and enlightens you."

After a moment's pause, he continued. "You see, Nephew, we are trying to get somewhere, to the heart of our true nature, perhaps, to the heart of something. And to get there requires work, the work of everyday life, certainly, but work on ourselves, as well. And we do both at once when we approach our work correctly."

"And that means, I presume," said young Mr. Patchet, "working in accord with human logic."

"Yes," replied the uncle. "And that is what I want us to discuss—the ethics that embody human logic. We will be discussing your experience at work, certainly—that is what brought us together—but our real topic is how to work in a way that matures and enlightens you. That's what too many people do not know how to do and yet, that is the real job. The irony is that your workplace profits most when you work in this way. This, however, has me ahead of myself. Up to this point—with this talk of ethics and human logic—are you with me?"

It was late afternoon. Young Mr. Patchet felt he knew in a general way what his uncle was saying, and he was eager to continue.

The two men decided to take the long way back to the house. They covered a lot of ground as the conversation moved from topic to topic. When they reached the house, they were chilled just enough to find the warmth of the wood stove soothing.

"Make yourself at home," said the uncle as he took his nephew's jacket. "As you can see, I've been preparing for your visit." Around the room were taped sheets of paper on which the uncle had written his thoughts. Ethic #1, Ethic #2, ...

"Some of what I have to say you may reject," he said. "That is fine. If so, then treat our conversation like a whetstone...as an opportunity to sharpen and refine your own ethics. However, to the best of my knowledge what I have to tell you is the truth and could not only save you trouble but could bring you great joy, as well. And that, my dear Nephew, I would like very much."

With that, they began; first reading and then discussing each ethic. It was a discussion that would change the course of young Mr. Patchet's life. Beginning in the early evening, it would be nearly midnight before they finished. Not until then—under a blanket of stars—would young Mr. Patchet return home.

"Work exists for the refinement of character."
E. F. Schumacher, economist

Ethic 1: The Organizational Ethic

*It is ethical to
serve, refine, and advance
the organization*
you have chosen to join.
It is unethical to
harm it.*

* for "organization" read: business, corporation, institution, family, or team, as appropriate.

"I have no problem with this," said young Mr. Patchet after reading Ethic #1, "at least within reason. It depends, of course, on what you mean by 'serve, refine and advance'."

"There's the rub, isn't it," replied his uncle. "If these terms are left undefined, people can say 'Fine, I already do that,' and each would mean something quite different."

"I mean ten quite specific things," he continued.

> **Ethic 1: Corollary 1**
>
> *It is ethical to learn everything you can about the organization of which you are a part (its overall purpose, the vision that guides it, its rules, practices and procedures, its parts, how they are connected, its history and status).* It is unethical to remain organizationally ignorant.

"Wait a minute, Uncle. I can't possibly learn everything about my organization. I could spend weeks and still not know everything. Maybe if I worked for a small company, but in my organization... Besides, I don't think they want me to know everything. And truthfully, I don't know that I care to."

"I understand," replied his uncle. "But you can learn enough to satisfy three very important requirements. First, you can learn enough to ensure that what you decide to do in your part of the organization does not make unnecessary trouble or work for people in other parts of the organization. You have an obligation to learn enough about the 'whole organization' so that you—through your actions—can help maintain and evolve it. Second, you can learn enough to ensure the ready detection of what are called 'conflicts of interest.' The more you know about your organization, the more likely you are to recognize offers, proposals and courses of action that are ethically and legally improper. You owe it to yourself as well as to your organization to avoid that kind of trouble."

"And the third, Uncle?"

"The third is crucial," he replied. "You can and must learn enough about your organization <u>to make sure that its ethics and values are consistent with your own</u>. It would sadden me a great deal were you to wake up in five or ten years only to discover that you had been 'serving, refining and advancing' an organization you did not believe in. This, my dear Nephew, you must never do."

"... be guided by this rule: <u>An employee cannot have too much information</u>." James A. Autry, The Meredith Corporation

> **Ethic 1: Corollary 2**
>
> *It is ethical to learn about the needs of those served by your organization (i.e., who they are and what they value) and, as well, about the needs of those within the organization served by your section or part.* It is unethical to remain ignorant of the needs of those you serve (whether you call them customers, consumers, clients, students or fellow employees).

"Taking care of your customers, right Uncle?"

"Yes," replied the uncle. "And it is important—obviously. Remember, the survival of your organization depends on its ability to meet the needs of those it serves. Finding out what really matters to your customers—both inside and outside the organization—puts you in a position to improve your products and services. Whenever you do that, you not only serve your organization, but you serve yourself. Your value to the organization grows."

Then, as an after thought, he added, "Let me remind you, Nephew, that one of life's most certain pleasures comes from fully and creatively serving others. You are the one—and this is the truth—who profits most in the serving."

"Renewal comes through genuine service to others."
Max DePree, Chairman and CEO, Herman Miller, Inc.

> ### Ethic 1: Corollary 3
>
> *It is ethical to perform your role (i.e., your job or duty) accurately, efficiently and pleasantly.* It is unethical not to do your job to the best of your ability.

"This might seem obvious," said the uncle, "and, in one sense, it is. Everyone knows that they should work to the best of their ability but the actual number who live up to this requirement is disheartening small."

"On the other hand," countered young Mr. Patchet, "maybe everyone is doing as well as they possibly can. Maybe, under the circumstances, on a day-in day-out basis, everyone is performing up to their limit."

"That's one way of looking at it," said the uncle. "But frankly, I think the evidence is to the contrary. People do as well as they are inclined to do, not as well as they can. And I'm not talking just about the so-called 'worker.' I'm talking about everyone, from the president of the company to the person on the floor. People get lazy, careless. They drift. You talked the other day about the willingness to settle. I agree. And, I would add, it is self-destructive. Either directly or indirectly, through the overall weakening of the organization you jeopardize your position when you fail to perform up to your ability."

"So, what do you think is responsible for this, Uncle? Why do we—I suppose it happens to all of us from time to time—why do we allow our performance to drift and vary so much?"

"It's forgetfulness," replied his uncle. "People have forgotten that through their work they reveal themselves. If they were to remember this, performances would be consistently higher because, in general, people think far better of themselves than their work would sometimes indicate."

"Nearly half the work force expends only the minimum effort needed to get by." Robert H. Rosen, from his book, *The Healthy Company*.

> # Ethic 1: Corollary 4
>
> *It is ethical to perform your role (i.e., your job or duty) in a fashion that does not add to the work, hardship or distraction of others unnecessarily.* It is unethical to make work unnecessarily harder for others.

"This is what seems rampant," commented young Mr. Patchet after reading Corollary 4. "And the reason for a lot of tension and resentment at work."

"Yes," replied his uncle. "And so much of it comes down to good manners."

"I was at the theater the other night," continued young Mr. Patchet, "and throughout the performance, the person seated behind me kicked and nudged the back of my seat. It was distracting, and angering."

"Yes," said the uncle, "there is that in various forms, a lack of thoughtfulness. Sometimes, however, we're just looking for ways of getting out of doing what we don't want to do. We distract ourselves by imposing ourselves on others. (And sometimes, of course, it's no imposition at all as they are as ready as we are to be distracted.) The result, however, whether we are conscious of what we are doing or not, is an organization with a deteriorating performance. As distractions increase, so too do errors; and as errors increase, quality and morale suffer."

"Morale, Uncle?"

"Yes, especially morale," his uncle replied, "because everyone wants their work to result in quality. Ultimately, we all want to be associated with high standards, even, if possible, with things that are outstanding."

"'Hassle' means that the people inside the company spend more time working on each other than they do making something happen..."
Philip B. Crosby, from his book, *Quality Without Tears*.

> **Ethic 1: Corollary 5**
>
> *It is ethical to speak fairly and honestly of organizational members: to say about them what you would say to them. The same applies to the organization as a whole.* It is unethical to engage in malicious gossip, ridicule, or derisive humor.

"This is one of the ways we dishonor ourselves," said the uncle, "whether we know it or not, and a sure-fire way to seed distrust in the organization."

"Wait a minute, Uncle, it's a way of lightening the load, too. A little so-called 'derisive' humor, what's the harm if nobody finds out?"

"It's a poison," his uncle replied. "Have you ever been the object of derisive humor? Or malicious gossip? Ridicule? It's humiliating. No. If you care about your organization—<u>and what are you doing there if you don't</u>—you say about others only what you are willing to say to them."

"Sometimes, Uncle, groups within the organization, just to give themselves a sense of unity, ridicule—if that's the word—or, in some sense, make fun of individuals in other groups. It's done as a part of the everyday chit-chat, a way, perhaps, of bonding."

"Let me be clear, Nephew. This corollary is not about gossip per se, not about relating informal news to friends and associates. It's about malicious gossip, ill intent. It's not about teasing good-heartedly or about playfulness. It's about ridicule. And it is not about the absence of humor or about taking away the opportunity to bond with others through humor. It is about derisiveness, about making others (who would not find it funny) the butt of the joke. In the end, it is about the examination of your motives and the adjustment of your speech until they are consistent with the requirements of a workplace marked by trust, directness and candor."

"…those little differences we have with our fellowmen, insignificant disputes, unbecoming conduct…petty gossip…; (a man)…should hold them at arm's length…and give them (no) place in his reflections."
Arthur Schopenhauer, from his book, *Counsels and Maxims*.

Ethic 1: Corollary 6

It is ethical to follow the rules. It is unethical willfully and knowingly to break the rules or to remain ignorant of them.

(NOTE: It is naive to think that rules are never to be broken. Therefore, it is ethical to make exceptions to rules, practices and procedures when such exceptions serve (or do not harm) the organization. And further, it is ethical to share the reasoning behind these exceptions so that this reasoning can be examined and refined and, so that others can recognize sooner when and where exceptions are appropriate. It is ethical to help others in the organization acquire the discernment that allows them to make exceptions to rules, practices and procedures when such exceptions serve or do not harm the organization.)

"Rules are rules, right Uncle? And yet, some rules are so ridiculous. Are they never to be broken?"

"No, of course not," replied the Uncle. "Rules are guidelines. They help define the organization, but they are not ironclad. There will be times when taking exception to them is appropriate. But that should be done only when there is a clear justification for doing so. Remember, the rules exist because they support fair and legal practice and, in the end, maximize organizational performance. To violate the rules, or to remain ignorant of them, is to threaten that performance."

"And the rule for breaking the rules?"
"I'm not sure there is one," replied his uncle. "I suppose it has to do with whether or not, in your judgment, a fair advantage or harmless convenience is being prevented by the rule, or a more ethical end obstructed. If not, you stay with the rule. If so, you break the rule and serve the advantage, convenience, or more ethical end. Whatever follows, you at least will have shown the independent judgment and, perhaps, the moral fiber from which individuals and organizations—over the long run—usually profit."

"Things change; and a man is foolish to act as though they didn't. He's just got to keep playing along according to the rules of the game. And they keep changing too." S. E. White, in his book, *Rules of the Game.*

> ### Ethic 1: Corollary 7
>
> *It is ethical to seek the correction, modification and/or revision of rules, procedures and practices that are inconsistent with the overall purpose and stated values of the organization.* It is unethical to accept—without attempting to correct—organizational practices that harm the ability of the organization to accomplish its purpose.

"The important thing," continued his uncle, "is that when you do discover a rule or procedure that is inconsistent with the mission or values of the organization, that you attempt to change it. It's your duty to yourself as well as to the organization. Otherwise, you leave the organization in a weakened condition."

"Because other people continue to follow the rule?" questioned young Mr. Patchet.

"Yes," continued the uncle. "And by so doing, they have their time and energy wasted. Rules or practices at odds with the mission send a damaging message. They announce that the mission doesn't matter enough to have rules, practices and procedures that are consistent with it. It's confusing and can cause resentment. On the other hand, by ensuring that rules and practices are consistent with the purpose of the organization, the work that is called for remains meaningful."

"Set things in order before there is confusion."
Lao Tsu, from the *Tao Te Ching*.

> **Ethic 1: Corollary 8**
>
> *It is ethical to create organizational improvements. These improvements may be in the form of or result in increased revenue, decreased costs, improved services, or an enhanced organizational culture.* But whatever the form or result, it is unethical not to help the organization evolve.

"More than anything else I want you to have a life of meaningful work," continued the uncle, *"of work that matters to you. The catch is that only you can provide it. You see, you generally get out of your work what you are willing to put into it. That's the truth. No one can make your work meaningful for you, not over the long run. Creating ways to increase revenue, decrease costs, improve services, or enhance the organization's culture—just like going to the trouble to update organizational rules and practices—are all ways of putting yourself into your work. You owe it to your organization to do these things and your organization profits, but so do you. Through your effort to make things better you strengthen your ability to create and to contribute. There's more joy in this way of working and more personal growth, as well."*

After pausing, he added: "I want you to promise me, Nephew, that in the future, when you find your work particularly empty, that you will remember this discussion; this notion that the fulfillment you seek in your work is largely yours for the making."

<u>The Law of Intention</u>: "You get out equal to what you put in."
Colin Wilson, English writer, theoretician and philosopher.

> ## Ethic 1: Corollary 9
>
> *It is ethical to protect and defend the organization against destructive influences (such as outside forces or internal decision-making practices that lead to fraud, libel or abuse).* It is unethical to remain silent in the face of perceived threats to the organization's survival.

"Wait a minute," said young Mr. Patchet, after reading Corollary 9. "I'm willing to do my part, but are you talking about whistleblowing?"

"All I'm saying," responded his uncle, "is that you have a vested interest in the survival of your organization. Whistleblowing has its place, but it is a last resort. It might never be needed if people would speak up as soon as they find reason for concern. The truth is most people can't afford to stand by as their organization is weakened by what they think might be illegal or unethical acts. They've got their families to think about."

"I agree, Uncle. It's just that it's a potentially frightening thing to do."

"I'll grant you that," replied his uncle. "That's why it is so important for people to speak up or in some way respond as soon as they detect the slightest problem. If everyone would do that, then all the harder for any one individual or, indeed, for the organization as a whole, to drift astray."

"And if you do discover some illegality?" asked young Mr. Patchet.

"You face it," said his uncle, "if you can. And you take your willingness (or lack thereof) to face it as a measure of your ability to put fear aside and act on principle."

> "Never, under any circumstances, knowingly cooperate with or aid any potential client or associate who is engaged in any way in a destructive enterprise. Be uncompromising in this even if it appears that lack of cooperation will lead to economic or physical disaster for you. This last possibility is almost always an illusion, induced by fear."
> John David Garcia, from his book, *Creative Transformation.*

> **Ethic 1: Corollary 10**
>
> *It is ethical to leave an organization whose purpose and values conflict with your own.* It is unethical to remain in an organization that requires you to violate your values or personal code of ethics.

"It's not for your sake alone, Nephew, that I include this corollary, but for the sake of the organization, as well. After all, the organization cannot reach its potential unless it is comprised of individuals who believe in it and who whole-heartedly support it."

"I understand that, Uncle, but what about those people who say, 'Hold on, I've got bills to pay, a family to feed. There's no way I can afford to leave this organization even though I violate my values and ethics by staying!'"

"I say," and here his uncle chose his words carefully, "I say, 'OK, maybe you can not leave immediately. But you can begin to leave. You created a way in—didn't you—and you can create a way out.' And, further, 'unless extreme circumstances prevail, 'you must try to create a way out.' The price of not doing so is too great. No one can serve for very long something they do not believe in without enormous mental strain. It is crippling. On the other hand, nothing so empowers a person as does the turning of a negative situation into a positive one. From this effort comes a lasting self-esteem."

"Produce what you can believe in." Rolf V. Osterberg, from his essay "A New Kind of Company with a New Kind of Thinking" in *The New Paradigm in Business*.

"Hold on a minute, Uncle. You're asking for a lot here."
"I'll put supper on," his uncle replied. "It will take a while to heat up."

"I know of men and women who have worked in companies, in factories their entire lives, doing things it could hardly be said they believed in—perhaps doing things they did not believe in, though they may never have taken time to think about it but even if they did think about it, doing it anyway because their family needed the money. Are you saying that they were unethical?"

"No, I am not," said his uncle. "Your family comes first. Sometimes one set of values must be put aside for another, the love and concern for your family may come before all else, especially in difficult or dire circumstances."

"On the other hand, if a person does find him or herself in work that violates their ethics or values, then yes, I am saying that not only for their own sake but for the sake of their family, they should find another way, another form of livelihood if they can. It may not be possible right away, or easy; but for the good of all concerned—the individual, his or her family, the organization and certainly, society at large—I believe that they must try to do so."

"At the same time, Nephew, every situation is unique. My primary concern here is with you and with whether you can move yourself past every excuse and every impediment that would have you violating these ethics. It's your happiness that matters most to me and I believe very strongly that your happiness, and your growth as a person, is most assured when you are working in accord with these ethics, Ethic #1 and the others we have yet to discuss."

Young Mr. Patchet stepped back to consider his Uncle's comments and the whole of Ethic #1. Only after considerable thought did he renew the discussion.

"If I look at Ethic #1 and its corollaries," said young Mr. Patchet at last, "it seems to me that I am being asked to take responsibility for my organization, to act, in a sense, as if I own it, which clearly, I do not."

"Yes," replied his uncle, "though I would put it differently. I would say that you are being asked to act like a person with choices, a person both capable and responsible. If you have elected to be a part of the organization, then serve it, advance to the best of your ability, behave as if it belongs to you. With that approach you are most likely to make decisions that benefit the organization and, in turn, yourself. If, on the other hand, you find that you do not belong in the organization and you lack the energy to 'improve' it by means of the various corollaries we have discussed, then Ethic #1 invites you to leave the organization. It invites you to find or create a situation you do like; one you can serve."

Ethic 2 - The Open-Mindedness Ethic[2]

It is ethical to be open to the possibility that your view is incomplete, capable of expansion and improvement. It is unethical to ignore information that could allow you and/or your organization to grow.

"One of the things that has astounded me, Uncle, is the number of people I come across at work whose minds have closed down, people of all ages. Mention another point of view, let alone a new idea or another approach, and they get visibly uncomfortable, even hostile. It's frustrating."

"I'm not saying I have better ideas," continued young Mr. Patchet. "I don't. But I would like to work in a place where ideas are welcomed. We get so stuck in our ways, our habits of thinking and doing. I'd like to work where the novel and unconventional doesn't pose a threat."

"There's a deeper point," his Uncle added, "one that has to do with the way people think. It seems to me that most people, even if their mind remains somewhat open, tend to think in only one of two ways. Upon hearing a new idea, they focus exclusively on its disproof, on why it can't possibly be helpful or relevant. The idea is examined in terms of whether it 'fits in' with what already exists. The alternative—and less frequently used style—is to try to see how the idea might fit in, to give it the benefit of the doubt, revising what already exists and enlarging it, if necessary, so that the potential of the idea or proposal can be examined. The first way aims to 'separate out,' the second, to 'bring in. Both are useful and in any given situation may be needed."

"And the benefit, Uncle?"
"The benefit?"
"Yes, the benefit to the organization or to oneself of a mind open to both ways of thinking?"
"Mental agility," replied his uncle. "The enhancement of one's creativity."

"...full unfoldment of creativity requires the ending of rigidity."
David Bohm and F. David Peat, in their book,
Science, Order, and Creativity.

> ### Ethic 2: Corollary 1
>
> *When seeking a more complete formulation or a difficult-to-find solution, it is helpful to ask others what they think. But it is also helpful to precede your own view with phrases that leave open the possibility that you may not be right, phrases like "As I see it now," or "My experience in these matters leads me to conclude…" Such phrases qualify the finality of whatever follows and leave room for creative problem solving.* It is unethical to speak so as to deny creative input from others.

"It is a matter of creating the proper climate," continued the Uncle. "Of creating a context wherein people feel safe enough to share their ideas without fearing censure. If that is done, then people will give you the best of what they know."

"You're not talking about eliminating stress, are you, Uncle? I've heard that people perform best when there is some pressure to do so."

"Of course not," replied his uncle. "But the stress will take care of itself, fluctuating in response to the demands of competition, profit, or the organization's effort to reach its goals. What I'm talking about is a climate of openness and safety, a climate where people feel their ideas are welcome and they are free to be involved. When extreme production pressures arise, it's the workplace characterized by this sort of climate that is in the best position to respond."

"And yet, won't there be times, Uncle, when a supervisor or manager will have to call the shots, will have to forego the niceties of asking for input and announce exactly what must be done and by when?"

"Of course, and the response the supervisor receives at that time will be all the timelier and more efficient if he or she has made, overall, a practice of being open and responsive."

"If we are open only to discoveries which will accord with what we know already, we may as well stay shut." Alan Watts, writer.

> **Ethic 2: Corollary 2**
>
> *It is ethical to be open to the possibility that you yourself, or some unknown factor, may be responsible—however minutely—for the undesirable events occurring in your organization.* It is unethical to presume absolute certainty concerning the failure or fault of others. Such absolute certainty can obscure or cut short the examination of other factors and lead to destructive action against individuals rather than to your own growth as a person or to improvements that benefit the organization.

"*Uncle, I sometimes think the biggest game at work is the 'blame game.' The amount of time taken up with it is startling.*"

"*Yes, and by actively seeking to affix blame, people distract themselves from the opportunity to examine their own behavior. They fail to realize that on occasion it is we ourselves who produce the undesirable events that come our way. After all, in an organization everyone is connected to everyone else and to the processes that make up the organization; everyone potentially connected to and contributing to the good that the organization does and also, sometimes, the bad. But instead of examining one's own contribution, if any, the 'blame game' continues. The result is that prejudices are confirmed, not dispelled. The mind closes as suspicion, and not personal responsibility is fostered.*"

"*Now, of course, actions against individuals may be necessary. Specific individuals may be sufficiently responsible for some undesirable or damaging event, and if so, then the proper sanctioning will need to occur. But by following the guidance of this corollary, we increase the likelihood that we will not miss the opportunity, should it exist, to make needed personal or organizational improvements.*"

"To become aware of what is happening, I must pay attention with an open mind. I must set aside my personal prejudices or bias. Prejudiced people see only what fits those prejudices."
John Heider, from his book, *The Tao of Leadership*.

Ethic 3 - The Deliberate Action Ethic[3]

It is ethical to choose consciously and execute deliberately specific actions that you believe represent the best of your discernible options. When the time to act has come, it is unethical not to do something.

Ethic 3

It is ethical to choose consciously and to execute deliberately specific actions that you believe represent the best of your discernible options even though you are not certain—indeed, can not be 100% certain—that the actions you have selected are "correct." When the time to act has come, it is unethical not to do something.

Tell me, Nephew, what does this ethic mean to you?"
"It means that I should proceed purposefully," answered young Mr. Patchet, "that when the time to act comes, I should act and not do nothing."
"Yes, exactly," responded his uncle. *"And why?"*
"Because, otherwise, I drift."
"Yes, because otherwise you drift."
"So, tell me, Uncle, what is so wrong with drifting? It has gotten me this far!"

"You were not hired to drift (nor were you born to drift)," replied his uncle. *"You were hired to be involved. That's one thing. Plus, you cannot learn nearly as much from drifting as you can from your effort to be deliberate. Deliberate acts are like investments, whatever the result you are at least wiser."*
"Plus, it would seem," added young Mr. Patchet, "deliberate acts imply a willingness to be accountable."
"Yes, indeed," replied his uncle. *"Accountable and, as some would say, 'pro-active'. No one appreciates problems that could have been avoided or opportunities that were missed because someone did nothing. In some ways, it's the difference between being asleep and being awake; to drift is to be asleep, to proceed deliberately is to be awake."*

"…only deliberate action…is distinctively moral."
John Dewey, from his essay, "Morals and Conduct".

Ethic 4 - The Feedback Ethic[4]

It is ethical to request, encourage and deliver feedback on all facets of individual and organizational performance. It is unethical to ignore, discourage or fail to give feedback.

"It's feedback that allows you to get where you are intending to go," said the uncle. "Without it, you are lost."

"Why then, Uncle, are some people so often afraid of it? Don't they want to get where they are going?"

"They do," replied his uncle, "of course they do. I suppose it is because feedback means evaluation. With feedback you learn how far off course you are, and the news isn't always good. So, feedback can mean change and change can mean inconvenience, trouble."

"But that only postpones the change, right? And makes a larger problem more likely down the road."

"Precisely," replied his uncle, "which raises another point. To be interested in feedback is to be interested in the truth, more interested in the truth than in personal convenience or in keeping things as they are. Feedback allows you to know the truth of your situation; to know if you are on or off course. With that knowledge you can accomplish your purpose, and you can help your organization accomplish its purpose. Without it, you and your organization are in the dark."

> ## Ethic 4: Corollary 1
>
> *It is ethical to request and encourage feedback on your performance, product(s) and materials from all individuals with whom you interact and/or who, in one way or another, receive your services whether they be inside or outside the organization.* It is unethical to ignore or discourage feedback.

"If nothing else," said his uncle, "it's bad business not to request feedback."

"Bad business?" asked young Mr. Patchet.

"Look," his uncle continued, "whenever you request or encourage feedback, you are telling your customers their opinions matter. Whenever you ignore or discourage feedback, you are telling them their opinions do not matter. It's the difference between honoring and dismissing those you are in business to serve."

"Plus, I suppose you would say, only with feedback can you get the information you need in order to serve your customers more effectively."

"Yes, exactly," replied his uncle. "That is what they mean when they say that customer needs, values, and satisfaction need to in part drive the refinement of products and services. When refinements are made on the basis of customer concerns (if it is possible and practical to do so), everyone's satisfaction increases and so, too, presumably, does the success of your organization."

"...no system can operate humanely without adequate feedback."
Philip Slater, from his book, *Earthwalk*.

> **Ethic 4: Corollary 2**
>
> *It is ethical to offer feedback to those from whom you or your organization receive services.* It is ethical to acknowledge outstanding performance, just as it is ethical to provide feedback to those whose performance or service threatens the optimal performance of you or your organization. In both cases, it may be unethical not to do so.

"Giving someone feedback can be very uncomfortable," said young Mr. Patchet, "especially negative feedback. For one thing, lots of people don't want to hear about something that is wrong and will blame you for bringing it up."

"I know," said his uncle, "but effectively giving negative or corrective feedback is one of the most important skills you ever acquire."

"Perhaps, Uncle. Though I would prefer almost anything to giving certain people negative feedback. It can be excruciating."

"It requires the development of a genuine concern for others," said the uncle, "while at the same time maintaining your allegiance to the organization. I know how hard it can be. But if you can give negative feedback sensitively, in a straightforward manner, without indictment, apology, or anger, then you can take away much of the recipient's excuse for 'blaming the messenger.' This takes self-control on your part, and maturity, but the development of these traits is your duty to yourself."

"Feedback is creative when its perception enhances the creativity of those who perceive it." John David Garcia, from his book, *Creative Transformation.*

> ### Ethic 4: Corollary 3
>
> *It is ethical to deliver feedback sensitively and to accept it graciously.* It is unethical to diminish the person to whom you are giving feedback or to punish the person from whom you are receiving it.

"Here's the subtle part," continued his uncle. "The feedback we give others can reveal as much about us and what we value as it does about the performance of the individual to whom we are giving the feedback. We may or may not be right about the importance of the issue on which we have chosen to give feedback. We may or may not have the whole picture. At the same time, the person giving us feedback may be right, he or she may be representing very well the best interests of the organization. Therefore, it is vitally important that we give feedback sensitively and that we accept it graciously because, in both instances, the feedback may be more about us than it is about the other person."

"A man cannot speak but he judges himself... Every opinion reacts on him who utters it." Ralph Waldo Emerson, from his essay, "Compensation".

Let's step outside before we sit down to supper," said his Uncle. "It's the last light of day."

The sun was setting across the hills where they had taken their walk and where young Mr. Patchet had played as a boy.

"There is a poet named Donald Hall," began his uncle, "who says that people suffer from 'work anger.' Not everyone, of course, but some. Work anger. It's a disease that can cripple you. And for most people, it's a matter of how they approach their work. Remember, what we are discussing here is a way of working, a way of creatively and ethically involving yourself with your work until you begin to see that the obstacles you face, many of them (not all, of course), are in you and that your real work is about what you are making of yourself. Hall calls that awareness, and the increasing absorption in your work that it makes possible, 'the paradise of work'."

Young Mr. Patchet was immersed in his thoughts. It had been a long time since he had treated his eyes to the play of gold and red across the landscape. A long time, too, since someone had gone to such trouble to inform him for his own sake—and here, on a topic so fundamental he was surprised he had not heard it all before. But he had heard it before, some of it at least, just not in this way. In some respects, he felt he was learning as much about himself, his hesitancy and his willingness to 'do what it takes' as he was about the nature of work.

Finally, when the last bit of light had faded, his uncle interrupted the silence. "Let's go back inside," he said. "Supper is ready and our discussion has given me an appetite."

Ethic 5 - The Truth-Telling Ethic

*It is ethical to tell the truth,
to be honest.
It is unethical to lie.*

> # Ethic 5
>
> *It is ethical to tell the truth, to be honest. Truth-telling allows the organization to know itself clearly and so to match its resources with greater precision to the demands of the moment.* It is unethical to lie. Lying creates misinformation, confusion and distrust, threatening your ability and the organization's ability to survive, adapt and prosper.

"No exceptions, Uncle?" asked young Mr. Patchet after reading Ethic #5.

"No," replied his Uncle, "there are exceptions. But they are not as common as some people think. Lying, or withholding the truth, usually is done for personal convenience, to avoid a problem that needs to be addressed or to gain an advantage. It's not justifiable under those conditions. Only if the person cannot be benefited by the truth are you justified in withholding it and such instances are rare."

"What if telling the truth does harm to another person—hurts their feelings unnecessarily—or puts them in danger?"

"Yes, of course," replied his uncle. "There are exceptions. Overall, however, the lies and half-truths told at work are told for the sake of personal convenience, for fear or gain, not because someone's life is at risk. It's lying—along with the discovery of those lies—or the withholding of a truth to which people believe they have a right that hurts feelings or puts lives in danger, not truth-telling. Often, even when we think we are justified in withholding the truth, we find, upon reflection, that we are not protecting someone else's feelings but our own. I'll grant you that there are exceptions to this ethic, to all the ethics, perhaps, but discerning those exceptions can be a challenge. Most people have a far greater capacity for the truth than our fear about sharing it sometimes allows us to think."

"And so, Uncle, when someone asks you a question are you compelled by this ethic to 'spill the beans,' to let it all come out?"

"Not at all. Some questions ask for answers that are no one's business but your own. In those cases, it is truthful and ethical to say that for personal reasons, or for the sake of your privacy, or someone else's, you do not discuss such matters, but you don't lie."

"So, you tell the truth with discernment, and you let the chips fall where they may. Is that the idea, Uncle?"

"Yes, in part," replied his uncle. "But you also tell the truth for your own sake, for the sake of your effectiveness and your own clear-headedness."

"Meaning?"

"When you lie," continued the uncle, "you have to keep track of who you told what. Otherwise, you run the risk of being found out. For that reason, memory and mental capacity—otherwise available—wind up being devoted to 'keeping things straight.' The result is that you have fewer of your own resources available for creative work. I don't know if the truth will set you free, Nephew, as some have said, but lying certainly restricts you, of that I am certain."

"All right, Uncle," said young Mr. Patchet with some resignation. "Still, I'm thinking about the discomfort involved in telling the truth; not always, of course, but sometimes. For example, when sharing a difficult, perhaps unwanted truth with someone whose performance is harming the organization, someone who you know will resent your effort no matter how carefully you proceed. Those are terribly uncomfortable situations."

"There is no denying it," responded his uncle. "Telling the truth, as in your example, can be very uncomfortable. It requires that you put fear aside or, at the very least, that you put principle above convenience. That's why truth-telling is so highly regarded, why traditionally it has been considered one of the central measures of ethical and moral strength."

"…my driving conviction is that all humanity is in peril of extinction if each one of us does not dare, now and henceforth, always to tell only the truth and all of the truth, and to do so promptly—right now." Buckminster Fuller, from his book, *Critical Path*.

Ethic 6 - The Pain-Directed Ethic

It is ethical to work first on the issue causing the organization (or your part of it) the most pain; and when that has been resolved, to work on the next most painful issue, and so on. It is unethical to ignore painful issues.

Ethic 6

In ongoing organizational development, it is ethical to work first on the issue causing the most pain, and then to work on the next most painful issue, and so on, in this way creating improvements in the sequence most likely to ensure not only survival but organizational health, as well. It is unethical to ignore painful issues. By ignoring painful issues, they are allowed to compound, threatening all the more the ability of the organization to accomplish its purpose.

After reading Ethic #6, young Mr. Patchet felt himself pull back. The discussion to this point had energized him but now, with this ethic, he felt divided; he needed a moment to survey his thoughts.

"Imagine it," said the uncle, not noticing his Nephew's withdrawal. "If tomorrow everyone in the organization worked on the issue that in their opinion was causing their area of the organization the most pain, within a week the organization would be a different place. Eventually, it would be a better place. <u>Avoidance of duty</u>. Nothing so backs up the lifelines of an organization or clogs its arteries quite like avoidance. And the sluggishness demoralizes everyone."

Young Mr. Patchet did not respond. He stood immersed in thought.

"What is it, Nephew?" asked the Uncle at last.

"I did not realize," began young Mr. Patchet, "how much of our discussion would be about fear. This ethic, for example. To follow this ethic means that you must do what you are afraid to do or at least, are disinclined to do; otherwise, you would have done it."

"There are those," replied his uncle, "who say that you cannot talk about ethics without also talking about fear, that fear is the reason we do not behave ethically."

"And you agree, Uncle?

"Sometimes," he replied. "But sometimes I think it is fear that drives us to behave ethically. I must tell you, Nephew, every time someone thought I was behaving bravely, it seemed to me I was merely doing the least frightening of my options. The consequences of doing anything else appeared more frightening."

"And courage?" asked young Mr. Patchet.

"Yes, of course," continued his uncle. "But what I am telling you is that the more you think about the ethics we are discussing—and what they ask of you in any given situation—the more irrational any other course of action becomes. The ethics we have discussed thus far, and the ethics we have yet to discuss, aim you in a direction that minimizes your difficulties over the long run, while at the same time promoting your growth as a person. To be sure, it's a direction that challenges you, but that's the idea... to exercise capacity and refine character. It's frightening to go any other direction; self-destructive and therefore, irrational. What we are charting here, I believe, is a sane course of action, and by following this course, the individual makes his or her organization saner, as well."

"All of this may be so, Uncle. I can see how it might be. I also see how it might be overwhelming. This ethic in particular, the notion of dealing with the issue causing my part of the organization the most pain or the most difficulty; quite honestly, I find myself shuddering at the thought."

"I understand," responded his uncle, "and yet, this is exactly what we want from the organization's leaders, its managers and supervisors. We want escape and avoidance stripped from their management style. We want them to deal with the issues that will make the organization a better place. So what if the issues are difficult! And so what if they are afraid to deal with them! It's their job! It's not until we see that it is our job as well, that we, too, are called on to adhere to the same standard—and we are if the organization is to realize its full potential—that we see how they might not do it all the time."

"Yes, Uncle, and yet, my reservation, the reason I say, 'I shudder at the thought', is that I've let one or two issues go for such a long time that the prospect of dealing with them now seems beyond me. They've become mountains and I'm not sure I have either the energy or the skill to climb them."

"I know," continued the uncle. "And maybe in such instances you do find that you must first acquire a certain skill or, through smaller issues, build up your strength before taking on the more serious issue, the one causing your part of the organization the most pain. But be careful, Nephew. This, too, can be a way of avoiding what must be confronted. It seems legitimate, and it may well be but remember that the painful issues are likely to compound so long as they are left unaddressed. They will become 'mountains', as you say, and it just might be that you have more skill and energy than you think you have. Sometimes we just have to 'jump in'. Once in, the requirements of the struggle to put things right takes over and we find that we are far more prepared—with both energy and skill—than we had thought."

> "…Everything we shut our eyes to, everything we run away from, everything we deny, …serves to defeat us in the end. What seems…painful…can become a source of…strength, if faced with an open mind." Henry Miller, Twentieth Century American writer.

Ethic 7 - The Free Choice Ethic

It is ethical to assume that within your organization all your behavior is freely chosen, that you are involved voluntarily. It is unethical to presume, unless extreme circumstances exist, that you are being forced to do anything.[5]

"I have you here, Uncle," said young Mr. Patchet. "No one knows for sure if we even have free choice. I've read the great philosophers, East and West, and they are quite divided on the issue."

"That is their luxury," replied his uncle. "You, on the other hand, cannot afford it. You must assume 'choice,' assume it as a part of your endowment. And further, I would say, you must assume that through your choices you are forever crafting your experience, creating it, with no one else finally to blame."

"And why, Uncle? I mean, I understand what you are saying, at least I think I do, but why does this strike you as so important?"

"Because, my dear Nephew, within the context of your organization, the organization you chose to join and from which you are free to exit, you are no one's victim. You are the victim, if at all, of your choices, and the beneficiary, as well. That is what I want you to understand or, perhaps I should say, that is what I want you to insist upon. Honor yourself with this view. Embrace it if you can. I believe it will serve you well. By trying to live up to this view, you will explore the very limits of your capability."

"Despite my initial protest, Uncle, I do think of myself as free, and as one who has choices. It seems to me that most people do."

"Many do, of course," replied his uncle. "And yet, try telling someone that they do not have to do what they are doing, that the work they are complaining about is work they are choosing to do, and you will hear an uproar, one excuse after another, about how they are not free, about how they have to do what they are doing, about how they have no choice. I don't want this for you, Nephew. It breeds the 'work anger' we discussed earlier. I want you to know that you always have a choice."

"But the choice you have may not be a good one, Uncle. For some people, the range of possible choices may be very limited."

"No matter how limited the range of possible choices—and that is an important point—pretending you have no choice is still worse," the uncle replied. "And further, whenever you do make a choice—consciously, deliberately—you invariably discover other choices of which you were unaware. Choice begets the discovery of—and capacity for—more choice, of that I am certain. At the very least, Nephew, you always can choose the attitude with which you decide to do something. That by itself will lead to the discovery (if not creation) of other choices, other options."

"And, by choosing to do what you have determined is yours to do," continued his uncle, "even though you can imagine other things you might prefer doing, helps you take the labor out of it. It eases the task, at least by degree. We eliminate a certain degree of impedance whenever we remember that with respect to most issues, what we have before us is voluntary and not mandatory at all."

Young Mr. Patchet considered carefully his uncle's comments.

"Shall I tell you how I became aware of this issue, Nephew? How the whole notion of choice came to me?"

"Please do, Uncle, though I think I understand the concept."

"Perhaps you do," replied his uncle. "Certainly, I thought I understood it when I was your age. But it is subtle. So, indulge me. Nothing is so at the heart of our discussion, or at the heart of human logic, as is this topic."

"When I wasn't much older than you, I worked for a very large organization. The pay was adequate, the working environment fine, certainly the people—many of them—were a pleasure to be with, but at some level I knew that this job was no longer for me. In any event, the instance I want to relate to you occurred in a meeting.

My boss was ranting and raving about the problems he was facing—with his boss, with colleagues, with competitors—to tell you the truth I don't remember the details. All I can say is that, in general, the experience was not different from what I had experienced on many other occasions, not pleasant perhaps but not unpleasant either. My boss wasn't blaming anyone; he was just letting off steam. What made this day different was what transpired in me."

"As he finished, or perhaps it was during one of his pauses, I witnessed an event that—looking back—was pivotal in my life. I'm grateful for it now, but at the time it meant many adjustments lay ahead."

"What I witnessed was my own very subtle decision to stop myself from saying what was right on the tip of my tongue, from saying what in the past had come so easily. I stopped myself from asking: <u>'How can we make this better?</u>' Instead of asking what we might do to eliminate the problem so that things would run more smoothly, I chose to remain silent. At that point, I realized later, <u>I was choosing—subtly perhaps but choosing nonetheless—not to be involved…in a sense, not to be there."</u>

"As time passed and as other similar 'choice points' arose, I again stopped myself from asking how we could make things better. I again chose not to be involved. Eventually, of course, through my choices, I had so removed myself from the organization that my boss called me in and encouraged me to resign when, in fact, <u>I had already done that months before</u>!"

"I was fortunate. I saw that I was doing this to myself. Had I not seen my own role in this I might have blamed my boss for my situation. How dare he! This is his fault! He is forcing me to leave! No, I had chosen to leave—he merely pointed it out. It began when I chose to stop myself from asking how we might improve things. My only regret is that I did not have the nerve to act on my own choices (or to choose otherwise had I, upon reflection, decided I wanted to stay)."

"In any event, Nephew, that—I believe—is one of the ways we do it to ourselves, in jobs, relationships, the entire course of our lives. Through hundreds of little choices, made daily, over weeks, months, even years, choices we know we are making, we take ourselves down a road which, when we wake up and see where we are, we scream, 'This is terrible! I never would have done this to myself. Someone else has got to be responsible!' ...when maybe, just maybe, in many instances (not all, of course), we took ourselves there every step of the way. Better to wake up to our own role in this, Nephew, our role as author or architect of our own experience. Far better. Unless I am mistaken, this is what is meant when the philosophers to whom you referred call on us to live a conscious life."

Bad Faith: "seeking to blame someone or something for what one has done freely oneself, ...pretending that one is born...determined... instead of recognizing that one spends one's life...making oneself."
From Hazel E. Barnes' "Introduction" to Sartre's
Being and Nothingness.

Ethic 8 - The Conscious Mistakes Ethic

It is ethical to eliminate conscious mistakes. It is unethical to engage in them.

> # Ethic 8
>
> *It is ethical to eliminate conscious mistakes.* It is unethical to know that what you are about to do is a mistake and to do it anyway.

"I have been in jobs," began the uncle, "where I have begun the day thinking to myself, 'This is a mistake!' And still I went ahead. No effort at all directed toward changing either my situation or my way of looking at it. In my view, Nephew, that is unethical."

"Why unethical, Uncle? Why not just a mistake?"

"Don't miss the point," replied his uncle. "Mistakes can be the most useful thing life sends our way. We learn from our mistakes; but conscious mistakes are different. They undermine effectiveness. You can't keep doing something you know to be a mistake and feel good about yourself."

"Like eating too many sweets," added young Mr. Patchet, "or having that last drink you know you should not have before hitting the road."

"Yes, like doing anything you know to be a mistake, from falsifying travel expenses to not checking the references of a new applicant, whatever it is. To know that something is a mistake and to go ahead and do it anyway is to choose failure, for yourself and for your organization."

Then, as an afterthought, his uncle added, "E. F. Schumacher, the great economist, said that 'work exists for the refinement of character.' If he is right, as I believe he is, then part of everyone's job is to reduce their number of conscious mistakes, because the refinement of character is measured—at least in part—by the reduction in conscious mistakes."

"It is by not doing what they already know they should do that companies get into trouble over quality." Philip B. Crosby, in his book, *Quality Without Tears.*

Ethic 9 - The Sustainability Ethic

It is ethical to consider the long-range implications of your decision-making and to make sustainability a guiding tenet. It is unethical to implement knowingly practices that ensure the collapse or diminished health of self, organization or environment.

> # Ethic 9
>
> *It is ethical to consider the long-range implications of your decision-making and to make sustainability a guiding tenet.* It is unethical to pursue short-term personal or organizational gain that ensures the collapse or diminished health of yourself, your organization or the environment.

"Do you know what a trap is, Nephew?"
"Of course, I do," replied young Mr. Patchet. "It's when a hook is baited with a frog or worm."
"Yes, exactly," replied his uncle. "It's where short-term pleasures or advantages are traded for long-term pains or disadvantages."

"In particular," he continued, "the kind of trap I want to talk about is the kind in which the individual enjoys immediate (and, in some cases, continuing) advantage from his or her behavior while the group of which he or she is a part experiences immediate or long-term disadvantages."
"Like polluting smokestacks," added young Mr. Patchet.

"Yes. In the short term, the factory discharges its pollutants into the air because it is cheaper than filtering out the toxins, but in the long run the air is polluted, and everyone suffers. A few people profit financially at the expense of the community as a whole."

"And, obviously," offered young Mr. Patchet, "that is not a situation that can be sustained."

"Right. Eventually, the opportunity for the few to profit is used up, or the unfairness of the situation forces some kind of corrective action. In either case, the situation cannot be sustained. A fellow named John Platt called these arrangements 'organizational or social traps,' and argued that they are responsible for many of the social and environmental problems facing us today."

"And so," affirmed young Mr. Patchet, "the importance of considering the long-range implications of your decision-making."
"Yes," replied his uncle, "for the sake of maintaining balance and avoiding burn-out, personally and organizationally."
"And thus, for the sake of the future. Right, Uncle?"

"Yes, for the sake of the future. This is the ethic that most encourages a future-orientation. It invites you to consider your legacy by considering what must be done now in order to help ensure the future you most desire for your family, your organization, your community."
"Economically desire?"
"Yes, of course economically. But also, socially and environmentally—one sphere cannot be considered without the others. We're talking about the big picture here."

"The problem, Uncle, is that you are asking people to forego their immediate gratification, to give up what is right in front of them, convenience if not economic gain, for the sake of something better down the road. Do you think that is realistic?"

"Perhaps not," responded the uncle. "And yet, when I think about it, nothing so moves me as does the willingness of the individual to sacrifice for the sake of a dream, or the parent's willingness to sacrifice for the sake of his or her child. That is why this is not unrealistic. Enlightened self-interest can be involved. Great things, meaningful things, never occur without discipline, without the foregoing of short-term pleasure or convenience for the sake of long-term gain. And everyone, deep down, wants to be associated with great and meaningful things. All of us want our lives to be meaningful. It therefore is in your interest, Nephew—and in the interest of your organization—to behave with the long run in mind. If there is inconvenience in the pursuit of your dream, or inconvenience in the pursuit of sustainability, then it is made up for by an increased sense of meaningful sacrifice, and by the knowledge—now felt—that you are living for something larger than yourself."

"...for are not ethics the subordination of selfish part to social whole?"
Camille Paglia, from *Sexual Personae*.

Ethic 10 - The Wind Harp Ethic

It is ethical to treat others as you would like to be treated, to "be the change you expect." It is unethical to do otherwise.

Ethic 10

It is ethical to treat others in and out of the organization as you would like to be treated even though you are not always so treated. It is unethical not to find appropriate avenues for the expression of your anger, resentment, and rage to keep from passing them on to, or taking them out on, others. It is unethical to engage in scapegoating.

"The Wind Harp, Uncle?"

"Yes, according to legend it is an instrument that existed during the Middle Ages. Presumably, you could affix it to the window of your mud and straw hut in such a way that wind, entering from one side, exited the other side as music. The Romantic Poets were taken with this notion and argued that we are all Wind Harps or perhaps could choose to be."

"We could be Wind Harps?" questioned young Mr. Patchet. "Uncle, I'm not sure... "

"Meaning," interrupted his uncle, "that it might be possible to develop enough character, or control, or presence of mind, that no matter what ill-wind happens to blow your way, you will be able to work with it, not passing your gathering anger, resentment or rage on to those who had nothing to do with it."

"Unlike the supervisor who treats the people in his department rudely just because he happened to be treated rudely by his supervisor."

"Yes," replied his uncle. "There's no 'kicking of the dog' here, or anyone else for that matter. The Wind Harp was seen as a device for ending the cycle of violence, a lovely and uniquely human idea."

"And who said, 'Be the change you expect'?"

"It was Gandhi," his uncle answered, "the great Indian leader. He said that or something very much like it and I was very taken with the phrase. It struck me as human logic, pure and simple."

"And profoundly demanding."

"Yes, of course, especially if you, like most people, consider yourself worthy of the basics, of courtesy, fair treatment, and respect."

"What is it that the organization gets out of this, Uncle," asked young Mr. Patchet, "other than a bunch of nice people?"

"The organization that embraces this ethic builds for itself a reputation for prejudice-free, non-discriminatory practice. Hiring, promotion, interpersonal and customer treatment, all are anchored to fairness. A reputation for fairness serves to protect the organization against attempts to diminish its name."

"And the individual?"

"The individual gets the same, Nephew, a well-earned reputation for integrity, for moral strength. But there's more. The Wind Harp Ethic, with its insistence on treating those in and out of the organization as you would like to be treated (whether they are customers or not) means that this ethic—and by implication, the entire code we have been discussing—cannot be embraced by organizations that have as their mission the destruction or diminishment of others. Unless you want that for yourself, you cannot seek it for others."

"Gandhi's human logic."

"Yes, Gandhi's and others," replied his uncle. "As far as I can tell, it is a notion common to many if not most of the world's great systems of thought."

"Ethics is a way, or the manner of interconnection of acts that makes human beings truly human beings." Watsuji Tetsuro's *Rinrigaku (Ethics in Japan)*. Translated by Yamamoto Seisaku and Robert E. Carter.

"And what are 'appropriate avenues,' Uncle? I see the point, of course. To hold those feelings inside, unreleased, is to invite all kinds of stress-related trouble, maybe even an eventual explosion."

"There are many avenues," replied his uncle, *"from daily exercise to hearty laughter to crying and screaming behind closed doors. Hobbies too, your artwork or meditation, anything that allows you to let your anger go safely, creatively. Therapy is one of the best ways because it helps you gain perspective as well as release. The important point, however, is that you find some way to release your negative emotions and to do so regularly. Otherwise, they can build up to the point where you find you are taking them out on others, or on yourself."*

"And when you take them out on others, that's what you mean by scapegoating?"

"Yes. That and more," replied his uncle. *"Scapegoating is the blaming of others for your discontent. It can take away the energy that you might otherwise use to change things. It's a violation of the Free Choice Ethic as well as of this ethic and it does tremendous damage. In addition to being a misguided use of personal energy, it costs the organization dearly with the various rifts it produces between individuals and groups."*

"Treat them all in a lofty manner lest they have cause to find thee weak."
John Dee, 18th Century Metaphysician

The two men stepped outside for the night air. It had been years since young Mr. Patchet had seen so many stars.

"What was it you use to say you wanted to be when you grew up?" asked his uncle after several moments of silence. "You were not much more than a toddler."

"I don't know," young Mr. Patchet replied, thinking it an odd question. "I suppose I said I wanted to be a fireman, or a policeman. A cowboy, perhaps."
"No, no, no, before that," his uncle said. "The very first thing?"

Young Mr. Patchet remembered. His family had laughed about it. "I said that I wanted to be like you and my father; handsome."

"Yes, exactly," replied his uncle. "It's a very deep desire, perhaps the first of every child, to be handsome like the loving and unselfish giants that surround him. And now, after all these years, during which time you, too, have become a giant, we finally can talk about it. As you now know, handsomeness or beauty is not something you are given but something you give yourself. It is self-bestowed. Therefore, if you still wish to be handsome, then conduct yourself in accord with this ethic. I know of nothing that so increases handsomeness as does conduct in accord with the Wind Harp Ethic."

Young Mr. Patchet's mind was racing. He was thinking about what he was experiencing as much as he was thinking about his uncle's comments. There would be time to examine the specifics later. Right now, he knew his uncle was sharing the best of what he knew.

"Come in," said his uncle finally. "It's late and we have more to consider."

"…character beautifies the body."
Confucius, 6th Century Chinese sage, from *The Wisdom of Confucius*.

Ethic 11 - The Personal Growth Ethic

*It is ethical to continue your growth as a person, to continue to increase your capacity to conduct yourself in accord with your ethics and principles.
It is unethical to stop growing as a person.*

> **Ethic 11**
>
> *It is ethical to continue to grow as a person, to continue to increase your capacity to conduct yourself in accord with your ethics and principles.* It is unethical not to continue the life-long process of personal/psychological development.

"Do you know of the notion that there are only two kinds of people in the world?"

"You mean winners and losers?" responded young Mr. Patchet casually.

"No," replied his uncle. "I do not mean winners and losers. I mean 'lovers' and 'teachers'.⁶

"'Lovers'," he continued, *"are those people who—through their interactions with you—introduce you to those behaviors, manners, qualities, traits, attitudes in yourself that you absolutely love. And 'teachers' are those people who—through their interactions with you—introduce you to those behaviors, manners, qualities, traits, attitudes in yourself that you do not love. From the point of view of this ethic, there are no other kinds of people in the world."*

"More human logic, I take it?" questioned young Mr. Patchet.

"Yes, most definitely," replied his uncle. "'Teachers' exist to help you identify what you need to work on as a person. Though you may dislike their 'teaching method,' they nevertheless offer you invaluable assistance in your ongoing effort to identify what you must learn if you are to increase your effectiveness, your wholeness or maturity as a person."

"Can the same person be both a 'lover' and a 'teacher'?"

"Of course," responded his uncle. "And with any long-term relationship, the person usually is both. This means that your organization, likely, is full of both 'lovers' and 'teachers'. Usually, we seek out the 'lovers' because we enjoy ourselves when we are with them. But the truth is, we can gain as much if not more from our 'teachers' if we can view our experience with them properly."

"Which means what, Uncle?"

"Which means we must try to identify the desirable skill, trait or behavior our 'teachers' are trying to teach us, the skill or behavior which, if acquired, will allow us to be ourselves around them, not in any way thrown off our game. In that way we turn our experience with them to our advantage."

"And to the advantage of the organization as well, you would say."

"Yes," replied his uncle, "as each member of the organization uses his or her experience with others as feedback on the direction that each should grow as a person."

"The organization as finishing school."

"Yes," added his uncle, "precisely."

"I'll tell you, Nephew, the individual who continues to grow as a person, who continues—increasingly—to behave in accord with the ethics we have discussed, serves their organization in more ways than they know. Not only do they present their organization with an increasingly reliable, effective and creative member, but they do so in a way that increases the optimism of all involved."

"Optimism, Uncle? I'm not sure I..."

"If you can turn your experience with your 'teachers' to your advantage, learning what you must to increase your ease and effectiveness when you are around them, then you make possible for your co-workers a very important conclusion; namely, that *if you can do it, so can they!* It is a conclusion you already will have reached for yourself. Optimism, morale, other intangibles—yours and theirs—are boosted by your effort."

"...the nature of work...properly appreciated and applied...nourishes and enlivens the higher person [and] furnishes [a] background for the display of values and the development of personality." J. C. Kumarappa, quoted in "Buddhist Economics" by E. F. Schumacher.

Ethic 12 - The Gift-Sharing Ethic

*It is ethical to utilize your gifts, talents, and unique experience on behalf of your organization.
It is unethical not to share your gifts, talents, and unique experience with others.*[7]

> **Ethic 12**
>
> *It is ethical to utilize your gifts, talents and unique experience on behalf of your organization. Through the expression of your unique gifts you may help your organization evolve and, in the process, acquire for yourself a greater sense of purpose and meaning.* It is unethical not to share your gifts, talents and unique experience somewhere, for the benefit of someone; and your organization does represent one place, if not the only place, where sharing your gifts benefits others.

"My assumption," began the uncle, *"is that everyone in the course of their life acquires a gift, some unique experience or knowledge that is essential to them, by which, in many cases, they identify themselves. And further, that the sharing of this gift—for the benefit of others—is one of the most deeply rewarding and meaningful experiences of their life."*

"And you are saying they should share their gift with their organization?"

"I'm saying that they must find a way to share their gift… with their organization if possible, providing, of course, it is valued, but if not with their organization, then somewhere, for the benefit of someone."

"If it is shared with the organization, then I guess you would say that the organization is strengthened because it thereby increases its creative wherewithal. And thus, perhaps, Its ability to address problems and to innovate to its advantage."

"That's the obvious way," responded his uncle. "But there is a more subtle way, as well. Whenever you accept a gift, the bond between you and the person from whom you are receiving the gift is strengthened. That's why you cannot accept gifts from some people, and why accepting a gift is serious business. It's the same with the organization. If an organization accepts a member's unique contribution, and then perhaps acknowledges that contribution in some meaningful way, then the bond between the organization and at least one of its members is strengthened. The organization is brought closer together. Yes, the organization is stronger because more of the talents of its members are being used on its behalf, but it is stronger as well because the bonds that hold it together are stronger."

"And the individual who contributes his or her gift?" asked young Mr. Patchet.

"The individual whose gift is received, who witnesses the acceptance, acknowledgment, and benefit of his or her gift, that individual feels infused, re-fueled, and, surprising as it may seem, he or she also feels lighter, more serene or perhaps joyful."

"Uncle, I'm trying to stay with you on this but I'm not sure..."

"It's like going to a party," said his uncle, interrupting. "It's not until the gifts are opened that the tension is released, and the fun begins."

"And what if you don't have a gift to give, Uncle?"

"Everyone has a gift to give," replied his uncle. "If their organization has no use for it, then the individual must find someone who does. At a very deep level, everyone is looking for the party where they can give their gift away, where their gift will be received and acknowledged, where they will see it benefiting others."

"Because when their gift is received, they feel renewed?"

"Yes, because they feel that they are fulfilling their purpose, at least a part of their purpose, and with that comes mental health. That's why the organization that utilizes the gifts, talents and unique experience of its members in its ongoing effort to grow and unfold becomes a more ethical organization. This cannot help but be so. Human logic. The healthier the members of the organization (and health is a matter of ethics as much as blood pressure and heart rate), the healthier the organization."

After a brief pause, his uncle continued. "Several years ago, I proposed to the leader of a large organization that all job descriptions in that organization be modified so as to reflect the human logic we've been discussing. All job descriptions, including his, I argued, should conclude with the following:

> 'And lastly, the individual holding this position should re-create it, he/she should make it new. The new version should include all that the organization found useful in the previous version while adding that which for the first time now is possible given the unique talents of the new job holder.'
>
> 'The process of re-creating this position should be done so carefully that the workplace never (or only very briefly) experiences the slightest decrement in overall performance.'

"It was my effort to announce through the organization's job descriptions that the organization did recognize each person's uniqueness and that—if possible—it wanted to benefit from that uniqueness by urging the individual to engage all of his or her faculties. It just so happens, I argued, that the individual benefits also from this effort. The footnote to my proposed change read:

> 'The re-creation of this position should be done <u>for the sake of one's own job satisfaction.</u> In so doing, the mission of the workplace will be furthered, and the organization as a whole will profit.'"

"And what was the response?" asked young Mr. Patchet.

"The leader of the organization said there was no way he could make this change. He said that his employees—Charlie, for example, who had been with the organization for twenty years—would think he was crazy."

"That was interesting, of course, since everyone knew that Charlie was one of the most sour and disgruntled people in the organization."

"It's not surprising though, is it, Uncle? You were asking for a lot. Some people might have found such a change to their job description threatening, having no idea at all what to do with it."

"Not everyone would answer the call or perhaps even understand the request," his uncle replied. "But some would. And who knows to what advantage."

"And then, I suppose you would say, other's—having seen the organization's support for those who did answer the call—might follow suit?"

"Yes. It's a process."

"So, what would you have had the leader of that organization say to Charlie?"

"I think he should have asked Charlie to go for a walk. And while on that walk, I think he should have said something like: 'Charlie, I no longer want the same-old-thing day-in and day-out for any of us. I want the organization to benefit from the best of what everyone knows, from their gifts and talents and unique knowledge. And I want you to be a part of that; I want you to look for ways to do that. Just give it some thought. But don't tell me you don't have any ideas for how to make things better around here. I wasn't born yesterday!'"

"You can assume you are fulfilling your purpose if you are in the process of turning your experience into products and events that bring advantage to others." Buckminster Fuller, 20th Century American cosmologist, inventor and poet.

It was late, time for young Mr. Patchet to leave. And though his head was spinning with ideas, he nevertheless wanted more.

"Human logic is the key," continued his uncle. "By behaving in accord with the ethics that embody human logic, you create for yourself what in some circles is called <u>a right livelihood</u>, a way of working that expands awareness, reduces suffering, refines character. That is what we have been discussing. By behaving in accord with the ethics of right livelihood, you put more and more meaning into your experience. Everything counts because everything is presumed a matter of choice, from what you do to how you do it. The organization profits when you are in this mode and so do you, since through your service you increase your capacity to serve, and to create, as well. The quality of your experience becomes increasingly yours for the making."

Young Mr. Patchet mulled over these thoughts as his uncle retrieved his jacket and prepared a snack for the road.

"So act as to increase the meaning of present experience."
John Dewey, from his essay, "Conduct and Morals".

"Where do you think we are going, Uncle?"

"Where are we going?" his uncle asked.

"Yes. This afternoon you said that only mature human beings could go on from here. That was the reason, you said, that ethics, or human logic, is so important."

"I think we are going to the stars, Nephew, if you want to know the truth. But that is a topic for another day. For now, it is enough to say that people are hungry for a higher standard. They want their organizations built on human logic because they want a 'right livelihood,' a livelihood with more joy, more meaning, and that can come only with an increase in awareness and commitment. And in my view, Nephew, nothing so increases awareness or reflects commitment as does the ongoing attempt to behave in accord with these ethics."

The two men walked outside. The night refreshed them.

"I keep thinking about the people where I work, Uncle. To tell you the truth, I don't think they are capable of doing what you are talking about."

"You can't know that," said his uncle, patting his nephew on the back. "Besides, the real issue is whether or not you can do it. And like we have already discussed, if you can do it, you'll be more optimistic about their ability to do it, and so will they."

"I know, Uncle, and I agree. But even so, I don't think that some of them would have any idea what you are talking about."

"Don't believe it, Nephew, though I must say I have heard that before, many times. Usually it goes like this:

> 'That's great', they say, 'I know what you mean but it may be too complicated...too deep...for other people in this organization, the people on the floor, for example, ...the guys in the shop...the middle and front-line worker. If you could dumb-it-up a little bit, make it easier to understand, then maybe... Otherwise, you'll be completely over their heads.'

"I always found this view offensive, Nephew, angering, because, as you know, I'm one of the guys from the shop. Besides, if those suggesting that I 'dumb-it-up a bit' truly understood what I was saying, they would know that the real issue is whether they can do it. If they would just focus on that, and not on how stupid or shallow everyone around them is, then they might provide an example that others could follow."

His Uncle was smiling. The two men embraced. Before saying good-bye, young Mr. Patchet expressed his heartfelt thanks and promised to return soon for another visit.

It was a long ride home and young Mr. Patchet was glad for it. Under a blanket of stars, he surveyed his uncle's argument. Human logic. The ethics of what his uncle called 'right livelihood'.

Years later, while reviewing the course of his life, a life rich with opportunity and meaning, young Mr. Patchet concluded that it was on this night, from his beloved Uncle, that he received the keys to his eventual good fortune; namely, the ability to give the best of himself over and over and to feel enriched and enlightened in return.

References

[1] "The Japanese word for ethics, <u>rinri</u>, which is of relatively recent origin (approximately one century old), translates roughly as 'human logic' or the 'way of being human'."
        Edwin M. Epstein
        Walter A Haas School of Business
        Un. of California—Berkeley

[2] This ethic is drawn from the work of John David Garcia. See his book, *Creative Transformation: A Practical Guide for Maximizing Creativity*, Noetic Press, Eugene, OR & Whitmore Publishing Company, Inc., Ardmore, PA, 1991.

[3] *Ibid.*

[4] *Ibid.*

[5] The view of choice elaborated here is offered as an assumption, perhaps the most useful of all assumptions, but an assumption, nonetheless. It should be embraced as if it is so, not as hard and unforgiving fact. There are, after all, many situations and many outcomes in life that are the result of outside and/or random forces—situations and outcomes where choice is not involved. There are victims in this world. The will of others can, and too often for many people does rule the day. That is why the discussion with Ethic 7 is limited to the organization we have chosen to join and are free to leave. By limiting the discussion to a context we have chosen to enter, we give ourselves less reason and justification for presuming that the power to affect our experience within that context exists outside of ourselves. We give ourselves less excuse for concluding we are victims when a closer examination would allow us to conclude that we may not be the victims we sometimes pretend to be.

[6] See the work of Ken Keyes, Jr., in particular his book, The Handbook of Higher Consciousness. Loveline Bks: Coos Bay, OR, 1990.

[7] Much of what is expressed by this ethic is drawn from the work of Garcia, see above.

Dr. Thomas is the developer of *The Ethics of Human Development Training Program.* The purpose of the program is twofold: first, to teach the Ethics of Human Development, the ethics that promote personal growth while at the same time furthering long term organizational success; and second, to build ethical and creative organizational cultures. Dr. Thomas has conducted Ethics of Human Deveopment Workshops in numerous organizations in both the United States and Canada.

To contact Dr. Thomas: dtec@cox.net
Website: davidthomasphd.com

Other Ethics of Human Development books:

Human Logic and the Theater of Everyday Life

The Ethics of Human Development: A Complete Guide

www.ingramcontent.com/pod-product-compliance
Lightning Source LLC
Chambersburg PA
CBHW071413290426
44108CB00014B/1798